Seasons
of the
Witch
LITHA ORACLE

Lorriane Anderson and Juliet Diaz

Illustrated by Tijana Lukovic

ROCKPOOL

Dedication

To the fans of this series who have been with us through the years: thank you so much for following this journey. You have made it possible for us to achieve this crazy dream of writing an eight-piece oracle deck series and we will forever be grateful to you.

A Rockpool book
PO Box 252
Summer Hill
NSW 2130
Australia

rockpoolpublishing.com.au
Follow us! **f** 🅾 rockpoolpublishing
Tag your images with #rockpoolpublishing

ISBN 9781922579768

Published in 2024 by Rockpool Publishing
Copyright text © Lorriane Anderson and Juliet Diaz 2024
Copyright illustrations ©Tijana Lukovic 2024
Copyright design © Rockpool Publishing 2024

Designed and typeset by Christine Armstrong, Rockpool Publishing
Edited by Lisa Macken
Printed and bound in China

10 9 8 7 6 5 4 3 2 1

Contents

About the authors — 152

About the illustrator — 154

Introduction

The wheel turns again, this time to Litha, also known as midsummer or the summer solstice. It's our first summer deck of the series, and in true fashion the deck we're working on is always the energy we need most at the time. It's funny how we never intend for that to be the case but it always works out that way. In this case we were calling in the energies of abundance, growth, creativity, power and success, all of which are naturally supported by the summer months introduced to the world through the summer solstice.

Seasons of the Witch: Litha Oracle was created to help you access these energies and begin or add to a practice of developing wealth consciousness. To experience wealth is not just about welcoming more money, but more of everything needed for you to feel whole. There are many pathways to experiencing abundance that will ultimately result in more money. It is our hope that this deck will unlock all pathways of prosperity for you, helping you to access the wisdom needed to see transformation in your life in the form of expansion, growth and, of course, more financial wealth too.

You will find that this is one of our more uplifting decks but that doesn't mean it won't challenge you. The 44 cards in this deck are tools encouraging you to face your blocks and the work needed to receive more bounty. They will require you to show up for yourself every day if experiencing more abundance is something you want.

Progress may seem slow at first, but we invite you to stick with it. Each time you choose positive or negative energy you inch yourself closer to your goals, but all good things take time. You can't exercise for a day and expect to lose 20 pounds or pick up your very first paintbrush and expect to paint a masterpiece, but with time and consistent effort you can welcome the energies of this deck into the rest of your life.

If you find yourself with this deck in your

hands it is your sign that you have already begun the process of doing this great work. At some point in the past your soul sent out a call for the right people and tools to help you develop your money mindset. This deck is a direct result of the desire of your soul, and indeed of souls all over the world, to experience abundance.

We can't wait to hear tales of how this deck has played a part in your journey, helping you to finally break through and have the success we know you've always wanted.

With love and gratitude,

Lorraine, Juliet and Tijana

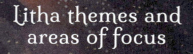

Litha themes and areas of focus

Abundance

Cleansing

Creativity

Fire energy

Growth

Inspiration

Motherhood

Power

Success

Vitality

Warmth

How to use the cards

Pulling cards

You may wish to establish an oracle-reading ritual such as lighting your favorite candles and incense, playing music or using a special space to do readings. Otherwise, spend a moment or two centering yourself by closing your eyes and taking a few deep breaths. When you feel calm, bring to mind your question then shuffle the cards and pull the card that feels right. You may experience a sensation such as a tingle or warmth when you have reached the card that is meant for you. Everyone experiences this differently, so if a card feels like the right one then trust that it is. Continue shuffling and pulling cards until your spread is complete if you are using one or until you have asked all of the questions you have. If desired, consult the guidebook for the card's meaning or use your intuition to guide you to the answers you are seeking.

Repeating element

If you are familiar with previous editions of the *Seasons of the Witch* oracle series you may have noticed there is one repeating element per deck that is featured in some way on every single card. The repeating element represents the heart and soul of the deck and is often the very first element we think of when beginning the creation process. Therefore, it becomes our guiding light as we develop the deck you now hold in your hands. In *Seasons of the Witch: Litha Oracle* that recurring element is butterflies.

The main energy we wanted to convey in this deck is abundance, but so few of us are gifted with the knowledge to be able to experience wealth consciousness. Most of us will have to do the work required to overcome our limiting beliefs, confront falsehoods about how we experience prosperity, learn to build confidence and believe all things are possible before seeing any real growth towards a positive money mindset. This is not easy work, but the results are well worth the effort.

We believe butterflies represent this transformative work beautifully. The process of a caterpillar becoming a butterfly is often romanticized, and in doing so it overlooks the incredibly difficult journey our little-legged friends must endure. They quite literally melt themselves down to rebuild themselves as something magnificent. They are willing to release their total identity to find freedom and to expand into their fullest potential.

That is our hope for you as well: that you will use this deck to release the blocks and crippling stories or habits that have prevented you from experiencing more abundance in your life. And not just money, but more love, joy, kindness, fulfillment, passion, creativity and peace and more of all things that bring the light back into your soul.

With each butterfly that catches your eye, let it be a reminder that even the smallest, seemingly untalented being can become something spectacular. Boring can become bold, cowards can find courage, poverty can develop prosperity and you can morph into anything you choose. *Seasons of the Witch: Litha Oracle* will be there to support as you do the work that will unlock your path to greatness.

Using the cards beyond Litha

This oracle functions in the same way as any other oracle deck and the meanings can apply to any situation no matter what time of year you use them. You may find the themes held within this deck are most apparent during Litha, or midsummer, but each person experiences energetic cycles in different ways. This deck was created to support you in finding more abundance, light, expansion and blessings, and who doesn't want more of those all year long? However, there are some natural times to work with this deck outside of midsummer such as when you are:

* doing money-consciousness work
* experiencing spiritual growth and evolution
* seeking an increase in finances or a promotion
* unusually happy and undergoing life milestones
* seeking more confidence
* desirous of experiencing more beauty and bliss
* ready to manifest the life of your dreams

Besides working with Litha as an oracle deck there are some additional ways to use these cards that are listed below.

Daily guidance or reflection cards

Pull one card every morning to set the tone for your day. Consider asking questions such as "What do I need to know today?", "How can I navigate this day successfully?" and "What kind of day can I look forward to?" You may also wish to pull a card in the evenings to summarize the day, asking something such as "What is today's take away?", "How did I operate at my best today?", "What do I need to release from today?", "What is something I should reflect on?" and "What needed my attention today that I've ignored?"

Guiding light cards

Each month, consider pulling a card for the energy of the month ahead then photocopy it, cut it down to size and place the copies where you can see them often. Doing so will remind you of the energy that is driving your spirit or something to be mindful of as you navigate the days ahead. Consider doing the same if there is a card in the deck that represents the intention you would like to manifest. Each card can serve as a mini vision board, helping to keep your goals front and center – and, of course, a photocopy of any of these cards would be fantastic on a full vision board as well.

Falling cards and reversals

Sometimes cards will fall from your deck when there is a message that really needs your attention. Honor that card, even if you've already pulled another card for your question. While we have chosen not to include reversals in this deck, a card might fall from the deck while shuffling and land in the upside down position from time to time. When this happens it means the message held within the card is especially important and you should take additional time to contemplate its meaning.

Litha card spreads

✦ ✦

Interview your deck spread: getting to know seasons of the witch

This spread is always included in these decks because interviewing your deck is a must-do practice and you should undertake it with every deck at least once. Getting to know your deck is crucial if you're serious about being an oracle-deck reader. The following reading sets the tone for the way your deck will communicate with you. Each deck has its own personality, sometimes even if you have two copies of the same deck. Have you ever heard someone say "My deck tells me like it is" or "My deck is always so comforting"? The spread outlined below will let you know how your deck speaks to you:

* **Card 1:** What personality do you have?
* **Card 2:** What is your strength?
* **Card 3:** What is your weakness?
* **Card 4:** How will the deck help you grow?
* **Card 5:** When should you call on the deck for guidance?
* **Card 6:** What is the best way to work with the deck?
* **Card 7:** What will your relationship with the deck be like?

Hydration spread

Use this spread to find more clarity or guidance about your question or situation. This is an excellent spread to use when pulling the Hydration card in a previous reading:

★ **Card 1:** How are you currently viewing your situation?

★ **Card 2:** What are your blind spots?

★ **Card 3:** How can you experience a deeper understanding of your situation?

★ **Card 4:** What action steps can you take for a positive resolution?

Farmers' market spread

Making a decision when you have too many options can be a struggle. Use this spread to help you see your soul's deeper desires and understand which option is best for you:

* **Card 1:** What do you need to know to make a choice about your situation?

* **Card 2:** No choice is still a choice, so what would happen if you chose nothing?

Additional cards: Pull one card for the pros of your option and one card for the cons of your option. Lay out an additional pro card and a con card for each choice that is available to you.

Insects

This spread is an excellent one to use monthly to see if there are any blind spots that are in immediate need of your attention:

* **Card 1:** What problem or situation needs your immediate attention?
* **Card 2:** Why have you avoided dealing with this problem?
* **Card 3:** What will happen if you continue to do nothing?
* **Card 4:** How can you resolve this issue?
* **Card 5:** How can you prevent this from happening again?

Welcoming summer spread

The shifting of seasons is a great time for self-reflection. Use this spread to discover your biggest lessons from spring and what you can expect for summer:

* **Card 1:** What is your biggest lesson from spring?
* **Card 2:** How did you experience the most growth?
* **Card 3:** How can you successfully shift from spring to summer?
* **Card 4:** What can you look forward to in summer?
* **Card 5:** What obstacle will you face and overcome?
* **Card 6:** How can you experience the best summer ever?

The money magick Litha cross

The Celtic cross was the very first spread outside of a past/present/future that I learned how to do, and it's often one of the first spreads beginner card readers are introduced to. In honor of it, I have included a revised version in every edition of the *Seasons of the Witch* oracle series. The money magick Litha cross will help you unlock any blocks you have towards reaching financial success. This spread uncovers the most obvious reasons you have not experienced more money as well as deeper motivations you may not be aware of:

* **Card 1:** What is your current financial situation?

* **Card 2:** What is your biggest obstacle when it comes to making more money? This card represents your optimum opportunity for growth when it comes to manifesting more money. This is the one card you should pay attention to above anything else.

* **Card 3:** How is your past influencing your thoughts about wealth? Curious to know how your upbringing is impacting your financial choices? This card is mostly related to beliefs picked up during childhood. You may wish to pull an additional card for each parent or parent figure to see how they specifically impacted your beliefs about wealth.

* **Card 4:** Where is your wealth consciousness headed? You may already be taking steps to improve your beliefs about money, and this card will give you insight into how you are growing in your wealth consciousness. If the card is undesirable, make plans to confront and shift this belief.

★ **Card 5:** What do you hope wealth will do for you? Every surface-level goal has a deeper desire. This card describes how you hope wealth will change your life for the better.

★ **Card 6:** What is your higher self trying to tell you about your financial beliefs? The message received here is a much deeper understanding of your limiting beliefs. This message might surprise you and awaken your mind to something you haven't considered before.

★ **Card 7:** What is your next positive step forward? This is an action you should take immediately for more positive results.

★ **Card 8:** How are you being influenced by external forces? Your community, environment and upbringing can affect your thoughts and beliefs about wealth in ways you may not be aware of. This card will help you to understand how social conditioning influences you and what you can do about it.

★ **Card 9:** What are you afraid will happen if you have increased wealth? A big part of money consciousness or lack thereof is fear. Find out what you're afraid of and stay open minded: you may find that what you most want is also what you most fear.

* **Card 10:** What is the outcome? This card describes what will happen if you take everything you read here into account. Doing this spread has already altered your future. If the outcome here is still less than desirable, take steps to put this advice into place and redo this spread in 30 days.

Litha
cards

Bike ride

+ 1 +

It is in the stillness and presence of the journey that you will find yourself exactly where you need to be.

1. Bike ride

Keywords: unhurried, enjoying the
moment, the long way home

*It is in the stillness and presence of the journey that
you will find yourself exactly where you need to be.*

Some summer days beg for a slower pace, those days when the sun is shining but there's just a bit of a breeze to keep you cool. Flowers are dancing in meadows, birds are singing along and a butterfly comes to rest on your shoulder as though to remind you to stop and enjoy the little things. Then there are days when you just don't feel like being rushed or productive, those days when you'd rather spend time doing what you love with who you love and when you take the long way home, not because you have to but because the world can wait.

Pulling this card is your sign to embrace this kind of day. It will appear when you are rushing through life without being present for it. You may recognize the symptoms of moving too fast: feeling anxious, doing a lot but accomplishing very little, a lack of focus and getting lost in daydreams, feelings of doubt or confusion about the future or a deep desire to do nothing. These feelings aren't manifestations of laziness or a lack of motivation; they are reminders that there is more to life than work and checking off another item on your to-do list.

Presence practice

This practice will bring you back to presence, allowing you to pull yourself in and be in the moment. Close your eyes for a moment and take four slow, deep breaths. With each breath you are going to focus on your senses:

* With your first breath focus on feeling. Is the wind embracing you, and do you feel the sun's warmth kissing your flesh?

* With your second breath focus on sound, and try to connect with nature sounds such as birds, water, wind or the crackling of a fire. Listening to the sound of your breath is also a great way to bring yourself back.

* With your third breath focus on sights, opening your eyes and looking around. Slow everything down as though you pressed the slow-motion button on life.

* On your last breath focus on combining feeling, sound and sight and creating an experience curated by you and the life around you: a slower, intentional and more intimate experience of presence.

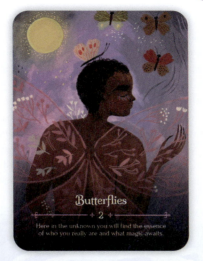

Butterflies

✦ 2 ✦

Here in the unknown you will find the essence
of who you really are and what magic awaits.

2. Butterflies

Keywords: breakthrough,
transcendence, profound change

*Here in the unknown you will find the essence
of who you really are and what magick awaits.*

The humble caterpillar melting down and rebuilding itself into a stunning butterfly is one of the most beautiful symbols of transformation the world has ever seen, and talk about an extreme makeover! A caterpillar essentially digests itself by releasing special enzymes within the chrysalis that dissolve its tissues into a soup of proteins that are then used to rebuild the body, forming its wings, legs and the rest of its anatomy. A caterpillar's willingness to completely break itself down is what leads to such profound change: it may be difficult, but it knows it has outgrown its current state and it's time to set itself free.

You are in the midst of a profound breakthrough and are about to transcend your understanding of who you were until this point. Spiritual signs come so rarely in the form of a huge flashing billboard, but in this case you can expect something truly dramatic to shake up your way of being. Whether or not this change is the result of a devastating event or a happy coincidence is unknown at this point. Either way, your life will look completely different a year from now as a result of what happens in the coming months. Pay special attention to synchronicities and dreams, as they are appearing to get your attention. They are your confirmation that what is happening is meant for you and you should continue to follow the threads. Additionally, this card is validation of a desire to make a significant life change and it means "Yes" when asking yes or no questions.

Cancer

3

Call yourself back from all space and time: to feel, sense
and reflect on the oceans of your presence within.

3. Cancer

Keywords: inner self, emotional
wellness, boundaries

*Call yourself back from all space and time: to feel,
sense and reflect on the oceans of your presence within.*

How are you doing? That is the question to ask yourself when the Cancer sun sign card appears in your reading. When was the last time you took a moment to check in with yourself, listen to your internal landscape and support your emotional needs? Cancer's mission is to teach you how to find your own little corner of the world where you can retreat to replenish your energy. It reminds you of the power of self-care and that your emotions can be potent allies when you take the time to listen rather than trying to suppress them.

Your emotions may offer you a deeper understanding about how and when you need to establish better boundaries, bring light to feeling overwhelmed and burned out, guide you to the things that bring you happiness or steer you away from what steals your joy. Every emotion has something to teach, and yours have been seeking an audience with you. Ask your emotions plainly "What are you trying to tell me?", then listen carefully because the answer may surprise you.

If you are reading about someone else, receiving this card could be a sign that they are not okay and could use some additional support.

Traveling self-scan practice

This is a check-in with yourself in which you focus on the emotions that are often left hidden or ignored.

Find a quiet space for some personal time to be with yourself, and sit or lay down with your eyes closed. Place one hand over your heart space or move your focus to your heart space, then take a deep breath, calm your mind and when you are ready say: "Emotions within, come forth one at a time." Take another deep breath, settle into yourself and ask: "Who wants to go first?" Allow your emotions to present themselves to you and witness how they show up and where they dwell in your body. You are not here to address them; you are here to acknowledge them and witness where they live and what they need to liberate you from them. Breathe slowly and stay calm; you are here to show compassion not only to your emotions but to yourself as well. Stay in this space as long as needed or pause and return later if it gets overwhelming.

This practice is excellent for seeing where you need to focus on self-healing or to address with someone such as a therapist, spiritual teacher, friend or family member you trust who may guide you.

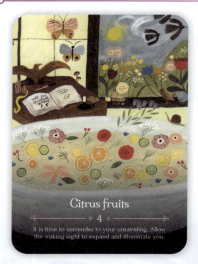

Citrus fruits

✦ 4 ✦

It is time to surrender to your unraveling. Allow
the waking sight to expand and illuminate you.

4. Citrus fruits

Keywords: spiritual opening,
cleansing, purity

It is time to surrender to your unraveling. Allow
the waking sight to expand and illuminate you.

The brightness, freshness and powerful cleansing properties of citrus fruits have appeared as a sign of your spiritual awakening. This is a powerful portal that promises the deliverance of the illusions you have experienced up until this point. You are literally waking up and beginning to question everything about your relationships, purpose and way of living. Old teachings, especially those to do with religion and spiritual beliefs, may begin to feel wrong or elicit doubts about whether or not you are actually receiving benefits from their guidance.

You may find that things naturally come to a conclusion when receiving this card: relationships drift away and you grow apart, a house no longer feels like a home or you feel it's time to move on from a career or job. These are intentional decisions that feel right rather than anything destructive or devastating; you are simply beginning to align with your soul and make choices that reflect this evolution. Ultimately, you will begin to feel more light and free as a result of this process and many people will begin to experience a deeper understanding of your soul's calling.

Clear quartz

✦ 5 ✦

The embrace of the shadows is gently lifting; light is needed now to nourish you.

5. Clear quartz

Keywords: clarity, light, amplification

The embrace of the shadows is gently lifting; light is needed now to nourish you.

Clear quartz is known as the master healer in the mineral kingdom and for good reason, as it has the ability to focus and direct energy – not just in the spiritual sense, but scientifically as well. It's used every day in technology worldwide from microchips and laser beams to microphones and radios, and the incredible gifts of amplification, clarity and focus are available to you and will help you to bring light to your own talents and higher states of being.

Crystals are attracted to those who need them the most. You have attracted the clear quartz card to encourage you to bring more light into your world in the form of positive energy. This card will guide you to put on your rose-tinted glasses and view the world with optimism and love. Speak positive affirmations, openly give compliments, go out of your way to experience joy and visualize positive energy swirling all around you.

You are in need of more harmony in your life and this card is your sign to do all you can to lift your vibrations. It's important to acknowledge your shadows, but be careful about getting stuck in the wounded healer archetype. Healing serves no purpose if you do not come back to the light to enjoy life with a higher level of consciousness.

Ignite your light ritual

In this simple yet powerful ritual you will learn how to ignite your light, which will help you expand and express intentional light from within. This ritual calls for the power of imagination.

Find a place where you can have some peace. Once you practice this enough times you will be able to do it just about anywhere, even in noisy and crowded places. Take a few deep breaths and quiet your mind. Place both your hands on your tummy and, when you are ready, close your eyes and imagine a candle living in the center of your body right where your belly is. Imagine reaching inside with both hands. You are holding a match in one hand and in the other a match book. Take a deep breath and light the match, then slowly move it to the candle and light the candle.

When the candle is lit, notice that the flame is a lovely bluish-white flame.

Move your hands out and take another deep breath, being still and allowing the warmth of the flame to embrace you from within. When you are ready, imagine the flame growing more prominent, brighter and warmer. Let it expand and fill your entire body, staying there for a few slow deep breaths, becoming familiar with your light and welcoming its embrace and power. If you feel ready to do so expand it outside of your body but keep it close, imagining it shaping out like a balloon around you. Fit it into the balloon shape, and feel it vibrating all around you. Sit with it, befriend it, set intentions and start a trusting relationship with your light.

Cloud scrying

✦ 6 ✦

Be still, for it's in the act of patience
that guidance is met with clarity.

6. Cloud scrying

Keywords: guidance, patiently
seeking answers

*Be still, for it's in the act of patience
that guidance is met with clarity.*

Isn't it lovely while out on a picnic on a summer afternoon to lie down on the grass and watch the clouds go by? Look closely and you will see images dancing about the bright sky. For some non-magickal folk this may seem like a fun game of optical illusions, but the clouds hold valuable insights and guidance for those in tune with the spiritual realms and willing to wait patiently for their wisdom to unfold.

Receiving this card is confirmation that your prayers have been heard and tells you to be patient as the answer presents itself. There is nothing more for you to do at this time except keep your eyes open for subtle clues and signs pointing you in the right direction. What appears hazy and formless at first can shift little by little until suddenly it becomes clear, offering the answer to a question or solution to a chronic problem. If you're seeking answers from or about another person, know that they are contemplating and will respond soon.

The shadow side of this card is attempting to force an answer: asking the same question again and again won't change anything but it could become irritating and frustrating to those on the receiving end. It doesn't matter whether you are directing your impatience towards spirit or someone you know; the answer will be given when the person is ready to give it.

Cloud-scrying practice

Cloud scrying is one of the first forms of divination that children are naturally drawn to. Many times we see what the clouds share with us in the form of fun shapes and images, but did you know you can communicate with the sky and receive responses to your questions? This practice is effortless; all it asks is for you to look up into the sky.

Find a place where you can be with the clouds in peace, and before you ask anything say "Hello", acknowledge the clouds' presence and take a few slow deep breaths. It takes patience, so don't expect the clouds to reveal something immediately. Sit with your question for a moment, then speak or think about it three times. Be patient and allow the magick to reveal itself to you.

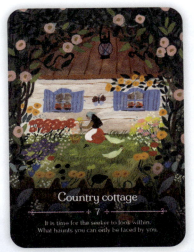

Country cottage

+ 7 +

It is time for the seeker to look within.
What haunts you can only be faced by you.

7. Country cottage

Keywords: sustainability,
self-sufficiency, independence

It is time for the seeker to look within.
What haunts you can only be faced by you.

Welcome to spiritual homesteading, the practice of finding independence, self-determination and sustainability for your soul's well-being. There's certainly no shortage of spiritual teachers, programs and tools on offer, including this deck you're holding, but the trouble with relying too much on someone else to guide you is that you lose the ability to stimulate your own healing and rewards. You are expecting someone else to show you the way rather than finding it for yourself.

You have pulled this card to encourage you to trust in your own guidance more than you seek advice and help from other people. You know what you need to succeed, you know what's not serving your highest good, you know what you want and you know what you need. What you're lacking is belief in yourself. Making a mistake or getting things wrong is part of the process, not a reason to quit or doubt yourself. You'll learn more from your failures than you will from your successes, and if nothing else they'll be your own: your choices, your mistakes and your determination to rise when you fall. Stay on the path you're on and have faith in your desires and ability to bring your rewards to life.

In a more practical sense this card appears when you are being a little bit too needy and should try to be more independent. It's fine to ask for help or want to experience life with others, but don't take anyone's time or resources for granted. You're more capable than you have allowed yourself to believe and you are fine to continue on this path alone.

Daisies

+ 8 +

There is a whisper of a glimpse of opportunities to fill your life with joy.

8. Daisies

Keywords: cheerfulness, pure joy, feeling better, love and care

There is a whisper of a glimpse of opportunities to fill your life with joy.

Daisies really are one of the happiest flowers: they are small but bright and seem to dance in the wind as though they haven't a care in the world. Often given to people who are sick or down, these little flowers bring a burst of cheer into your darkest days. Receiving them is a reminder that someone loves and cares for you and took the time to make sure you're doing okay.

Someone is thinking of you when you receive this card and would love to hear from you soon. They have wondered whether or not you're okay, or perhaps are hoping you're thinking of them as well. This card can mean a happy reunion is on the way, especially if someone specific popped into your mind. Reach out and see if there is an opportunity to reconnect with someone who could bring a vast amount of joy into your life. If someone reaches out to you, be sure to reciprocate the interest even if your last encounter ended on a sour note. Daisies are sometimes given as a sign of lasting love and friendship, so give things another chance.

Daisy abundance spell

This spell is a summer favorite of ours. Not much is needed to make spell work: the essential part of the spell is your intentions. You will need water in a bowl and a few daisies.

With a spell like this we recommend keeping your intentions to a max of seven. With each daisy flower, bring it close to your lips and whisper an intention into it then place it in the bowl of water. Place the bowl out in the sun or by a spot with sunlight. Leave it out for three days, and on the third day after the sun goes down you can dispose of the flowers by placing them on the earth. Make sure to thank the earth.

Farmers' market

+ 9 +

Remember to distinguish abundance from
wholeness. Choose wisely and intentionally.

9. Farmers' market

Keywords: abundance of choices,
farm to table (source to spirit)

*Remember to distinguish abundance from
wholeness. Choose wisely and intentionally.*

There is something magickal about seasonal eating and living farm to table; food is never fresher than when it's pulled directly from the earth. Sadly many of us do not have access to our own gardens but, fortunately, farmers' markets are becoming more common as people seek to return to a slower way of living. Each market offers far more than your traditional grocery store, from heirloom varieties to unique hybrids created by knowledgeable farmers.

There are many paths for your question or situation but not all paths will lead to success: each option offers a different flavor and may prove to be something you don't enjoy. Choose carefully, being mindful that the option that appears to be perfect may be hiding something underneath such as a perfectly formed tomato with a worm inside. When you are faced with an overwhelming amount of choices, lean on your higher self to guide you to the right answer.

Your spirit is connected to source, God, the greater intelligence or any other name you use to identify the divine. The answer is always available to you but, sometimes, your ego attempts to rationalize choices that should be made from your heart and soul. You may wish to spend time in meditation or communing with the earth in stillness for more guidance, or consider using the farmers' market spread in the Litha card spreads chapter for expanded awareness.

Check in with spirit prompt

This journaling prompt is one that I often go back to when I need to check in with my spirit and quiet the noise in my mind so I can allow spirit to lead me. For this exercise you'll need some paper and a pen or pencil.

Prepare by finding a quiet space and calming your mind. Take a few deep breaths, and when you are ready ask your question and allow yourself to write out all the thoughts that come to mind, even the unrelated ones. Once you have done that go to a different page, ask again and this time add: "Only my spirit may guide me." Without forcing thoughts in, allow yourself to record what naturally wants to be shared.

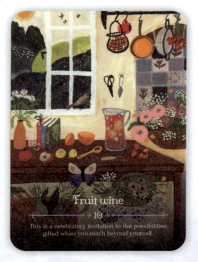

Fruit wine

+ 10 +

This is a celebratory invitation to the possibilities
gifted when you reach beyond yourself.

10. Fruit wine

Keywords: celebration,
invitation, breaking the ice

*This is a celebratory invitation to the possibilities
gifted when you reach beyond yourself.*

It's time to get out there and be social, to make new friends, build relationships and invite people along on your journey. Your chances of success will increase tremendously with the help of others. If you are seeking love, consider asking friends and family to make introductions or set you up on a blind date. If you are starting a business, seeking a partner who shares an interest in your plans may be the missing piece. Perhaps it's too much to go it alone, so having someone to share in the hardships as well as the successes can reduce the feeling of being overwhelmed you've felt on your own.

This card can also represent the presence of a kindred spirit, someone who understands you as though you were the same. There is the promise of lifelong kinship and a mutually beneficial pairing of support. The sense here is that you have found your folks and are experiencing the sense of coming home.

The shadow side of this card is feeling left out or left behind. Sometimes people grow apart or life gets in the way and it isn't as easy to spend time together anymore, which doesn't have to mean the end of a relationship but may be a sign to welcome new people into your life who can fill some of the void. Open your heart and allow different attachments to form. You never know when you've met the next addition to your soul family.

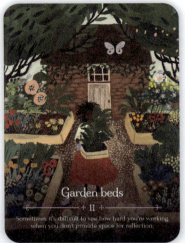

Garden beds

11

Sometimes it's difficult to see how hard you're working
when you don't provide space for reflection.

11. Garden beds

Keywords: working smarter,
resourcefulness, evaluating progress

*Sometimes it's difficult to see how hard you're
working when you don't provide space for reflection.*

Having a home garden is hard work, but there are ways to work smarter and make the most of the spaces you have with the use of garden beds. They raise your garden up, making things a little easier on your knees, help to keep critters out, allow you to control the soil content, reduce weeds and provide more growing space. It's a much easier way of setting up your home garden, especially if you are a beginner who doesn't have the know-how to tackle more challenging growing areas. Will it guarantee success? No, but it's always a good idea to work smarter, not harder.

This card questions how productive you have actually been. Are you doing a lot of busy work but achieving very little? Are you taking extra steps or making simple mistakes that are easily avoided? Take a look at your progress to determine whether you are actually making any progress; you could be wasting your efforts on something that isn't worth your investment. If you're happy with where you are, consider how you can be more methodical in your approach. Now might be a good time to hire an assistant, implement a system to increase input or consider eliminating something so you can focus all your energy into something else.

Drawing this card can also mean you're wasting a lot of time trying to learn skills when you could enroll in a class or work with someone who has the experience to help you cut through a steep learning curve.

Self-reflection mirror practice

It is no surprise that you work harder than you have to due to a hustle culture, trying to survive and pay the bills and having no space planned into your daily routine for self-reflection. Self-reflection should be integral to your life, whether you're an entrepreneur, working a nine-to-five job or are a stay-at-home parent or guardian. Reflection allows you to see and pinpoint where you are overwhelming yourself and allows you to adjust and address those issues. You will need a mirror you can stand up or sit on a flat surface, although a handheld one will work fine.

In this practice the power comes from having a conversation with yourself, from communicating with yourself. Try to do this at the end of the day, as in this way you can review your day and adjust as needed for the next day. For example: "This morning it took me so much time to write my newsletter. What caused this to take longer than anticipated? How can I be better prepared next time? What would help to have in place for a smoother, more efficient creation of my newsletter?" That is just an example, but you can honestly discuss anything in your day.

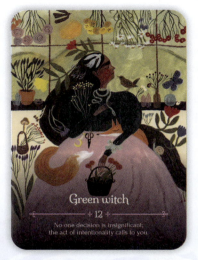

Green witch

+ 12 +

No one decision is insignificant;
the act of intentionality calls to you.

12. Green witch

Keywords: consequences of your actions,
mindfulness, interconnectedness

No one decision is insignificant;
the act of intentionality calls to you.

A green witch is in tune with nature, sensing the connection between herself and all living things. She speaks to plants, animals, the skies and rivers, hearing their guidance and sorrows, taking just enough for her needs while bringing awareness to the ways humans have negatively impacted the planet. Knowing how she treats the earth is reflected in how she treats herself, and how she treats herself is likewise mirrored in the entire collective consciousness.

Green witch is here to remind you to be mindful of the consequences of your energy. The words you speak, the way you view yourself and others as well as the actions you take have an impact on all of humanity. If you're cruel to someone that person may go on to harm themselves or others. If you hide your light from the world because of low self-worth or shame then you rob others of the chance to love and appreciate the gifts you were sent here to share. What you say and do matters even if you can't see the immediate cause and effect of your choices, and what you don't say and the ways you don't show up also have consequences.

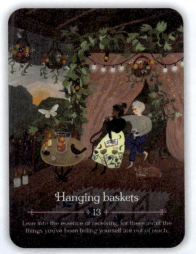

Hanging baskets

+ 13 +

Lean into the essence of receiving, for there await the
things you've been telling yourself are out of reach.

13. Hanging baskets

Keywords: attraction, beauty,
learning to receive

*Lean into the essence of receiving, for there await the
things you've been telling yourself are out of reach.*

Nothing says welcome to a warm, beautiful home full of cheer better than hanging baskets. Their delicate beauty attracts all sorts of other pretty creatures from every shade of hummingbird to butterflies and bees. When you receive this card it invites you to let your beauty be on display for the world to see. Don't worry about whether you're pretty, slim enough or have sufficient money, a good job or the right kind of talent. Everyone is beautiful in some way, and you are no different.

You may not believe that, thinking you've been passed over or that people simply don't notice you, but ask yourself whether that's true or whether your energy is closed to the attention. Do you duck your eyes when you see someone attractive rather than meeting their gaze? Do you blend into the background at parties, choosing to play the role of wallflower, or are you bright, vibrant and eager to mingle with friends and strangers alike?

No one can enter your house if you don't open the door. Learning to receive is as much about putting yourself out there as it is about accepting what is being offered to you.

Heather

+ 14 +

You are worthy, my dear. Silence the noise that strips you of your peace.

14. Heather

Keywords: peace of mind, protection of dreams, worthy of admiration

You are worthy, my dear. Silence the noise that strips you of your peace.

Rest easy, my dear; your dreams are protected. You may have felt worried that your plans have been foiled or that a recent bout of competition is going to derail your success. There is no cause to fear this recent attack because, although annoying, it is confirmation that you are worthy of admiration and those attempting to defeat you are projecting their own insecurities and fears that your light will dim theirs.

Pay no attention to the noise unless they are absolutely negative. You may have to stand up for yourself here and there but, otherwise, much of what you are experiencing is a whole lot of bark and no bite. Do not let anyone else's criticism plant doubt in what you have worked so hard to achieve. Keep your mind trained on your vision, establish boundaries and remember that you have gotten yourself this far and you can go as far as you dare.

If you are experiencing doubts you can always try on someone's comments to see if they hold any truth. To do so is a healthy form of self-awareness as long as you do it with honesty. If for some reason you do find a criticism to be true, know that it is well within your ability to confront and overcome any shortcomings. All people have faults, but that doesn't mean those faults have to prevent you from achieving your goals. Thank the naysayers for bringing this to your attention and then do what you do best: evolve.

Heat wave

+ 15 +

There is something ominous being
illuminated by the flames that await.

15. Heat wave

Keywords: seek shade, challenging
circumstances, getting burned

There is something ominous being
illuminated by the flames that await.

Please understand that the situation you have inquired about is potentially catastrophic. You should seek shelter immediately, as this is a clear sign that things will to come to an end and prolonged exposure could result in devastating consequences. The events that have led up to this point are not serving you in any positive way and, in fact, you might feel some effects already.

Stay vigilant in the coming days and weeks. This card is the most ominous of the deck and could mean your situation has already reached a critical point. In a reading about money it could signify financial loss or hardship. For career, it could mean the sudden loss of a job, dramatic changes in the workplace or escalated troubles with a co-worker. In love relationships you might experience a breakup or betrayal, and for health perhaps unexpected concerns or fallout from some poor habits that are contributing to your lack of well-being.

As a final note, the effects of this card are challenging, but you can choose to lean into these changes and make the best out of the rubble.

Heirloom tomatoes

+ 16 +

Enter into the depths of intimacy, where the
seeds of your desires will be nourished.

16. Heirloom tomatoes

Keywords: love, passion, lust

*Enter into the depths of intimacy, where the
seeds of your desires will be nourished.*

Heirloom tomatoes bring the promise of new romance for love seekers and renewed passions in an existing relationship. It goes beyond anything physical, entering into the depths of intimacy that is only accomplished by a deeper understanding of each other. Lust is born out of suggestive glances, feathery touches and whisper kisses teasing at something much more sensual.

If this is not something you're experiencing, consider seeking fresh ways to introduce more play into a relationship, romantic or otherwise. It's just as important to experience love for yourself as it is for a lover. Are you making time for your passions? When was the last time you acted on your lust for anything, not just a person but also a goal, purchase, food or location? This card guides you to give in to the need to spoil yourself and those around you. Everyone wants to be wanted and feel loved, including the universe. The extra affection goes a long way in stocking the seeds of desire, and you will find that the energy you give is also the energy you receive.

Bloody tomato love spell

This spell is fun and a beautifully intimate experience with magick. You can do this exercise for self-love or the love of a partner, friend or family member, or even for a passion and career. It will help to rekindle a fire and amplify love that is already present. You will need one whole tomato and a small jar or glass.

Cut the tomato into parts and remove but retain the seeds. Place the pieces of tomato over the jar and squeeze all the juice into the jar while thinking of your intention. Continue this with all of the pieces, making sure to also put in the skin of the tomato left in your hand. Take one tomato seed, set that same intention into it and place it in a jar. With the following seeds set intentions for anything that you feel needs to be released or amplified to help with the primary intention of the spell. For example, my main intention is to love myself better. In the seeds I can set intentions of being more consistent with hydrating, making time for movement, making space for rest and eating nourishing foods.

Leave the jar open and place it on your altar or in a safe place where it won't be disrupted for three days. Each day, go to the jar and speak your main intention over it. On the fourth day you may dispose of the jar and its contents however you like.

Herb crafting

17

Allow your roots to dive into the depths.
Your spirit calls for grounding.

17. Herb crafting

Keywords: gratefulness, grounding,
connecting with the earth

Allow your roots to dive into the depths.
Your spirit calls for grounding.

You are receiving this card because you are being called to get grounded. Energy is always moving around you and has an effect, and it can take its toll if you aren't careful. You could find yourself being swept away by the hustle and bustle of other people's emotions. You might recognize the signs of carrying stray energy in the form of intense feelings that do not seem to have an origin. The best way to reduce this influence is to ground your own energy, allowing you to find your roots and replenish your spirit.

Spending time alone, especially in nature, is advised. If you are reading this now it's likely you're an empath or a highly sensitive being who needs solitude to reconnect with your own energy. Being an empath is a wonderful gift but, like all things, must be exercised in moderation because you are not just picking up energy from others: they are also taking energy from you. Too much of this exchange can cause you to feel depleted, depressed and anxious, blocking you from achieving your own goals and attaining positive well-being.

Additionally, pulling this card means you are not ready to receive the answer to your question. Your spirit is too depleted at this time and needs to be repaired before making any additional attempts to move forward. Consider working with herbs to get more balance.

Grounding practice

Grounding can be done in many ways yet is often left out of people's practices. You should consistently ground, preferably daily and especially when working with magickal workings, spiritual practices and so on. This grounding practice is simple and effective.

While standing or sitting, raise both your arms to the sky with your pointer fingers out. Imagine your fingers illuminating with a brown light, almost like dirt. Trace this light around you by bringing your arms back down, circling from the top to the sides and then to the bottom, fingers still pointed. Once your fingers are pointing down, shoot the light into the earth. Travel with it as far down as you can and find a place to tie the light like a bow or shoelace, then slowly take a few slow, deep breaths and feel the pull coming in from the core of the earth. Release any tension, stress, fear and worries into this thread of light, giving it to the earth. Make sure to thank the earth and carry on with your day.

Horse

+ 18 +

Unsure of how to break out of your cage, spirit shares strength through acts of liberation.

18. Horse

Keywords: freedom, regality, confidence, strength

Unsure of how to break out of your cage, spirit shares strength through acts of liberation.

Horses are meant to be wild and free, which is why they are such powerful creatures that are capable of running for long distances and over different terrain. It's not uncommon to hear tales of having to 'break' a horse when attempting to domesticate a wild one. How sad it must be for a horse to go from roaming endless landscapes to being confined to a small box inside a barn. If a horse remains bound for long enough it may fail to see when the opportunity presents itself to run back into the wild.

When the Horse card gallops into your reading it could be a sign that your spirit is broken and you have lost your sense of regality and strength. You may feel stuck, stagnant, bored or stuck in a rut, unsure of how to break out of your cage to find more passion and excitement. Dig deep and reconnect with your sense of freedom. Remove the shoulds and supposed to dos from your perspective and follow your heart and instincts. The beauty about being free is that you can change your mind: if you go one way and find that doesn't work simply shift directions and try something else, never apologizing for not being caged.

Hummingbird

19

The winds beneath your wings are shifting and if you don't pay attention you may lose flight.

19. Hummingbird

Keywords: swiftness, adaptability, pivoting

The winds beneath your wings are shifting, and if you don't pay attention you may lose flight.

Hummingbirds are small but mighty with wings that can beat almost 100 times per second. They can travel great distances and change direction in an instant with smoothness and grace. You, too, are being called to be more flexible when Hummingbird enters your reading. The current path you're on isn't suiting your needs and it's time to consider some additional options or, at the very least, a new approach. Think about what is and is not working for you and how you can use this information to bring clarity to your question.

This card can also mean your situation is evolving rapidly and you are not keeping up with these changes, which can cause you to feel overwhelmed. If you are unwilling to adapt it may be time to consider whether or not this is the right path forward, because the world will pass you by if you hold on too tightly to outdated methods.

If you are reading about another person, receiving this card is a sign to speak up against someone who is too rigid in their thinking. You will continue to see stagnation unless all involved are willing to be more flexible.

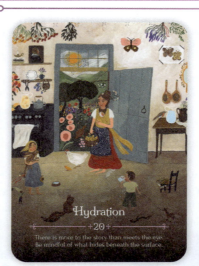

Hydration

+ 20 +

There is more to the story than meets the eye.
Be mindful of what hides beneath the surface.

20. Hydration

Keywords: basic nourishment, foundational
healing, source of the problem

There is more to the story than meets the eye.
Be mindful of what hides beneath the surface.

Ever had dry skin in the summer? Between sun rays, air-conditioning, salt water and chlorine your skin can take a brutal beating. You can increase your moisturizer, of course, but that is only treating the symptoms and not the problem. While environmental influences increase your chances of having dry skin, proper hydration is half the battle. Getting enough of this foundational healing by just drinking more water will have a significant impact on not only your skin but your body's overall wellness.

Spiritual well-being is similar. You may be attempting to manifest a large goal or heal an old wound but are focusing on the symptoms when there is a much bigger problem driving the external manifestations you're experiencing. Poor beliefs about self-worth may prevent you from attracting more love or wealth. A deep-rooted fear of new experiences may hinder your plans to travel more or chase after a dream, or you could find that troubles in a relationship are the result of a long-forgotten childhood wound. Additional information, understanding or healing is needed before this situation can come to a conclusion. Put on your X-ray glasses and look beyond the surface of your problem or question, because there is more to the story than meets the eye and you have only just begun to peel back the layers.

Insects

⁘ 21 ⁘

Vigilance is necessary at this time.
Heed the warning.

21. Insects

Keywords: pests, obstacles, vigilance

Vigilance is necessary at this time.
Heed the warning.

Pests such as insects and rodents can quickly spiral out of control if left unattended, wreaking havoc on your hard work and destroying your harvest. Sometimes it happens right under your nose, the destruction only becoming visible when it's already too late. Vigilance is necessary for the good of your crops, otherwise what was a small problem can be the cause of something truly devastating.

This is your warning that something is quickly getting out of hand and requires your immediate attention. A larger problem is avoidable, but only if you take steps now to get things under control. This situation may have drifted below your radar but there are signs of what's going on lingering in the back of your mind, or it could be something you haven't wanted to deal with and made a conscious choice to avoid. Small obstacles are par for the course, and while annoying they're easy enough to manage with proper consideration and care.

Typically you'll know exactly what this card is referring to, but feel free to pull additional cards or use the insects spread on page 17 if you're still unsure.

Lemonade

+ 22 +

Make the most of your situation by opening
your mind to new possibilities.

22. Lemonade

Keywords: making the best
of things, silver linings

*Make the most of your situation by opening
your mind to new possibilities.*

+ 85 +

We all know the phrase that when life hands you lemons you should make lemonade. It's a colorful way of telling you to make the best of a bad situation. Sure, lemons may not be very sweet but that doesn't mean they're worthless. Many of the world's best creations were born out of sorrow, frustration, and broken hearts. The need to make the most out of very little opens your mind, forcing you to consider what else is available to you now.

Sometimes, despite your best efforts things don't work out the way you'd hoped and you're left sifting through the pieces of what could've been. When someone betrays you or leaves you behind, you lose a job or a plan falls apart it can be easy to find yourself giving in to feelings of self-pity and grief. Don't allow it to take root. It's time to regroup, opening your mind and heart to what's possible. Channel all of the energy you're putting towards your sorrow and redirect it towards discovering something even greater.

Lemonade ice-cube spell

This spell is perfect for anyone who wants to sweeten up a situation or experience or life in general. You will face many hardships in life, and transmuting that into something that serves you is a powerful act within itself. You will need some lemonade, an ice tray and a jar or glass.

Pour the lemonade into the ice tray mindfully and slowly. As each cube fills, make sure to pray, chant, whisper or whatever you feel called to do to set the same intention into each cube. Leave in the freezer overnight, then the next day place the cubes into the jar. Pour fresh lemonade into the glass while setting your intention into the lemonade going into the glass. Stir the contents of the glass to match the number of cubes you placed in the glass – if you put in seven cubes then stir seven times – clockwise to amplify or bring in or counter-clockwise to let go or release.

Drink the lemonade in a peaceful space, preferably outside in nature, and enjoy the magick unraveling all around and within.

Lightworker

÷ 23 ÷

The transmutation of shadow is needed when seeking the light that guides you.

23. Lightworker

Keywords: soul alignment, following passions, transmuting shadow

The transmutation of shadow is needed when seeking the light that guides you.

When a light creates a shadow notice how the light doesn't dim as a response. It continues to shine even though the shadow is there, looming in the background. Light cannot avoid shadows any more than you can avoid people who are mean, rude, unsupportive or lacking vision. Shining your light doesn't mean everyone will love you; it means you're turning on your light so the people who can and will love you in the way that you need to be loved can find you.

Shining your light doesn't take much, simply a commitment to follow your passions and embrace the things that bring you joy, excitement and a sense of wonder. Your soul falls into alignment a little bit more every time you follow what's in your heart. There is no need to fear the hows, whys or what ifs: if a desire has made its way to you it's because spirit has already given it to you and is waiting for you to receive this gift.

The right people, place and opportunities will seek you out, providing you with the necessary resources to achieve your dreams. When you listen carefully your soul will tell you who is right and who is wrong, who can support you and who cannot. Don't worry about the shadows in the background: they can yell and intimidate, stare and complain but they do not have the power to stop your light from shining.

> *You don't get to tell people how to love you;*
> *you get to choose if you want to participate in*
> *the way they love.* — Iyanla Vanzant

Mermaid

✦ 24 ✦

*Let the allure of the mythical siren seduce
your curiosity. Magick awaits.*

24. Mermaid

Keywords: allure, seduction,
embracing desires

*Let the allure of the mythical siren seduce
your curiosity. Magick awaits.*

There are many legends about the mythical sea creature known as the mermaid. Among them is the alluring call of her song, said to enchant sailors so she can drag them to the bottom of the ocean never to be seen again. The assumption is that she drowns them in the sea, but what if something much more magickal and fantastical is happening? Maybe she opens up a whole new world that only the few who are brave enough to follow the call are able to experience.

The things you are attracted to are not a mistake or flights of fancy. They represent things that are meant for you and hold the key to more happiness, your purpose and ways to live your best life. If you are captivated by something, allow yourself to be pulled down into the depths of its seduction. It can be scary to follow a passion not knowing what waits for you on the other side, but the best things in life are often the things that scare you the most yet make you want to dive in.

Money magick

25

It is in limiting beliefs that magick goes to die.

25. Money magick

Keywords: wealth consciousness,
enough to go around

It is in limiting beliefs that magick goes to die.

Litha is all about abundance and growth, making it an excellent time to work on wealth consciousness. To have a healthy attitude towards wealth means knowing there's enough to go around for everyone. The universe and everything in it is unlimited; there is no end to the prosperity you can experience. Every person has the ability to be very affluent if their consciousness is tuned to the vibration of wealth.

How do you know if you have a strong wealth mindset? If your response to your potential to be prosperous was "I doubt it" then you are sabotaging your ability to manifest an increase in finances. You can never manifest something if you don't believe you can, and this card has appeared to you because it's time to do the work needed to eliminate self-sabotaging beliefs about finances.

There are common beliefs about money being evil, that people who have it are bad people, you don't have the right education or experience to generate wealth or you aren't the kind of person who could make that kind of money. With just a little bit of research I guarantee you can find someone who had very similar circumstances to you yet is living the life of their dreams.

This card is nearly always about money, but when it appears in a love reading it can mean your financial situation plays a significant part in your relationships. It may indicate fights about money or that you need to be in a stronger financial situation to attract the kind of partner you wish to have.

Stuffed-pepper money spell

Spells impact your mindset, and it's the repetition of practice and setting of intentions that allows you to rewire the way you think to bring about an outcome you desire. For this spell you will need one green pepper, three bay leaves, a pinch of cinnamon, green yarn, string or ribbon and some salt.

Cut a hole into the side of the pepper. Set intentions of money abundance into each of the bay leaves and push them through the hole in the pepper, then pour the cinnamon into the hole while calling in amplification to your intentions. Replace the cut piece of pepper, holding it in place by wrapping the yarn around the whole pepper. While you wrap, speak or think of your intentions. Sprinkle the salt over the pepper to seal the spell and place it on your altar or in an undisturbed place for three days. After three days you can dispose of the pepper however you like.

Mulch and manure
✦ 26 ✦
Hardships are coming to an end;
the seeds you sowed will be blooming soon.

26. Mulch and manure

Keywords: improving circumstances,
ability to hold more

Hardships are coming to an end;
the seeds you sowed will be blooming soon.

Mulch and manure downright stink. It isn't pleasant to work with but it does serve a very useful purpose: in gardens it helps to improve soil conditions and increases the dirt's ability to hold more nutrients and water. Of course, manure is the result of animal waste and there's nothing glamorous about that, but the results are undeniable. Brilliant flowers, ripe fruit and a plethora of summer veggies make the muck and smell worth a little bit of discomfort.

The obstacles you have lately faced are slowly improving your circumstances. The soil you were planting your seeds in before wasn't rich enough for your goals to thrive. You may have attempted to increase your finances, find love, change jobs or experience more peace in your life only to find your hard work spoiled again and again, and when that happens too many times the benevolent universe steps in to fill your life with fertilizer in the form of challenges, changes and losses that will ultimately result in new, fertile ground.

The good news is that your hardships are coming to an end and you will see sprouts shooting up very soon. In the meantime, do your best to understand the lessons your fertilizing period has taught you because you'll have to start all over again if you don't learn how to maintain what you're growing.

Paper boats

✦ 27 ✦

Stay afloat and don't tilt too much.
A lesson awaits you.

27. Paper boats

Keywords: sending blessings, receiving
good fortune, giving and receiving

Stay afloat and don't tilt too much.
A lesson awaits you.

✦ 100 ✦

A wonderful midsummer practice is to craft paper boats, fill them with flowers and blessings then send them off on rivers, lakes and streams. Whoever finds them will be blessed with good luck and fortune. It's a beautiful practice that teaches the art of giving and receiving.

Abundance is a two-way street: to give there must be a recipient, and to receive you must be willing to accept. One cannot exist without the other. There is no shame in sharing or accepting, and you will find yourself experiencing both sides of the coin many times over. Share your time, resources and skills when you are in a position to do so as you never know how a gift that is given without expectation can change someone's day, even going on to impact them for a lifetime. Each time you give, you deposit a karmic coin that will make its way back to you when you need it most.

If you find yourself on the receiving end, do so without feeling guilty for needing a helping hand. Allowing others to repay their fortune in kind to you is not a sign of failure or weakness but is one soul doing their part to uplift another and, in turn, lift up the greater consciousness. It all flows back into the unlimited stream of love, the universe's cache of kindness. Celebrate your turn in fortunes, being sure to pay it forward when you're back on your feet.

Peonies

✦ 28 ✦

It is time to reap your rewards.
Settle in for a ride with Lady Luck.

28. Peonies

Keywords: all-around good luck,
protection, increased blessing

It is time to reap your rewards.
Settle in for a ride with Lady Luck.

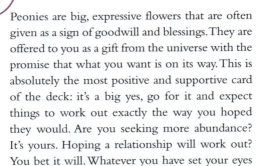

Peonies are big, expressive flowers that are often given as a sign of goodwill and blessings. They are offered to you as a gift from the universe with the promise that what you want is on its way. This is absolutely the most positive and supportive card of the deck: it's a big yes, go for it and expect things to work out exactly the way you hoped they would. Are you seeking more abundance? It's yours. Hoping a relationship will work out? You bet it will. Whatever you have set your eyes on is making a beeline straight towards you.

Don't be afraid to ask for what you want, as you are likely to receive it right now. It's not just the universe that's in a giving mood. You may get a free coffee just because, a favor at work, an offer to skip ahead in a long line and more. Allow yourself to receive this upturn in good fortune and don't question the reasons behind it. It may seem sudden and unusual, but you have planted seeds of gratitude for quite a while and you are finally reaping the rewards.

Rewild

✦ 29 ✦

Let your soul's garden grow wild, setting yourself
free and allowing mysteries to surprise you.

29. Rewild

Keywords: liberation, salvation,
being untamed

*Let your soul's garden grow wild, setting yourself
free and allowing mysteries to surprise you.*

Each person on this planet has genius hiding within them waiting to be unleashed, and that includes you. However, to access this inherent talent you must learn to let yourself be free. Brilliance isn't bound by convention, expectation, perfection or even rules; your genius needs space to experience all versions of itself. You are being called to let your soul's garden grow wild: don't be so quick to tidy up your corners or clear out the unwanted.

Weeds are also plants, many of which such as dandelion are supportive and nurturing to the body. Your spiritual weeds can offer you nourishment and guidance to help you better understand yourself. Your hardships and shortcomings may unlock a clever idea or inspire you to create a masterpiece. A shifting of your soul's cycles may bring light to ways you could experience more freedom and joy. Talents are often unlocked out of struggle and necessity and a willingness to let your soul lead you.

When this card comes to your reading it is asking you to follow where you are being called to go. Don't question the journey or the meaning, as this is simply your spirit's way of untaming you and sending you back to the wild so you can experience yourself in the freest way possible. You may feel called to go on a physical journey to a new land or it could be purely symbolic, requiring you to let go of who you thought you were or who you think you should be. Consider journaling about how you would express yourself if you had no rules to follow, people to make proud or expectations to live up to.

Roses

✦30✦

The soft petal felt upon your flesh is
ready to release her thorns.

30. Roses

Keywords: divine love, lasting
relationships, support

*The soft petal felt upon your flesh
is ready to release her thorns.*

Few symbols represent love more than the rose. Its delicate petals in pretty shades meet prickly thorns and sturdy stems, much like love in the real sense. A rose is beauty intertwining with the occasional pain, all in an enduring dance of sharing your life with another.

Roses in your spread symbolize an eternal love that has the potential to stand the test of time. It may not be fast or especially passionate but it is solid and supportive, affectionate and endearing. It's the kind of love that reinvents itself, like a rose turning into a dried flower and expressing its beauty in a completely new way. If you are in a relationship your partner is reliable and prefers to express themselves in practical ways rather than grand romantic gestures. They're more likely to fill your car with gas or take out the trash than to whisk you away to Paris, but you'll never have to question their loyalty. If you're seeking love this card reminds you to consider someone who may not be the most attractive or interesting but will be a soft place for you to land and rest your head through the good times and bad.

If your reading is about someone outside of a romantic relationship, receiving this card is confirmation of their devotion to you or a sign that they are okay and you don't have to worry about them. They will find the help and support they need. The same can be said for you if you're experiencing difficult times: help is on the way in the form of a supportive friend, mentor or family member.

Releasing rose bano

Rose is a powerful nurturer, and a simple rose bath to help you release what is no longer serving you while gently embracing you is perfect when you draw this card. You'll need a red candle, a handful of rose petals and one tablespoon of honey.

Fill the bath and light the candle. While doing so, think of the scent of roses. Sprinkle the rose petals slowly over the bath water then get into the bath and take a moment to ground into the warmth of the water spirit embracing you, the rose kissing your flesh and the scent of the roses filling your spirit. When you are ready, pour the honey into the bath water and ask honey to bring sweetness into your bath experience. Allow rose to gently travel with you into the emotions, thoughts or spaces you wish for her to guide you with.

Rot and decay

+ 31 +

It festers when left in the shadows;
bring it to life by giving it away.

31. Rot and decay

Keywords: cycles of life and death,
sacrifice for the greater good

It festers when left in the shadows;
bring it to life by giving it away.

Flowers can't bloom forever and even the summer experiences death, decay, and the need to sacrifice small parts for the health of the whole. It may seem like a waste on the surface but Mother Nature knows what she's doing and nothing dies in vain. Some fruits and vegetables will fall to the ground and rot, their sacrifice offering nourishment that makes for the most fertile soil.

The more fruitful your life is, the more you have to sacrifice. With abundance also comes the need to shed what is weighing you down, has been forgotten, or wasn't sweet enough for your harvest. Rot and decay reminds you that abundance doesn't mean you need to have everything for that would no longer be abundance but greed. Rather, it means you have more than enough for the way you wish to live. If you find you are carrying too much, receiving this card is your sign to leave something behind, in service of your greater good.

Consider how you may be spreading yourself too thin, focusing on things you aren't passionate about, or holding onto old ideas that are no longer facilitating your growth. Don't allow the need for "more" to weigh you down, in fear that your good favor will run out or that there won't be another chance. There will always be another season of harvest.

Scavenger hunt

+ 32 +

What you thought was hidden
is hiding in plain sight.

32. Scavenger hunt

Keywords: hiding in plain sight, new
perspectives, considering other options

*What you thought was hidden
is hiding in plain sight.*

The makings of a great scavenger hunt means hiding your items in plain sight but concealed just enough so that they aren't obvious and require a few quick passes with the naked eye. You can go it alone, but often working in pairs or teams proves more fruitful because different people bring different opinions, each one seeing things from a unique point of view.

Often the answer to your question or solution to your obstacle is right in front of your eyes, requiring little more than a change in perspective. Holding on too tightly to something – identifying with a particular career, idea, relationship or opinion – causes tunnel vision, whereby you choose only to see your version of the story. There's always another way, a different path or a deeper understanding. Looking at the same thing from a fresh angle can reveal the treasure that was there all along.

You may find yourself with this card when you are too focused on only one outcome or solution to your problem, refusing to look left or right or to consider someone else's ideas about how to proceed. Are you really sacrificing anything by letting go of your feelings and ideas about this situation and, if so, what if that sacrifice leads to something even more magnificent than you originally wanted? Be careful to make space for others to share their wisdom and experiences, and don't be afraid to challenge your ideas of right and wrong or you'll only end up with one egg in your basket or perhaps nothing at all.

Stargazing

+ 33 +

It takes a lot of courage to reach for the stars
to expand the self, but it is possible.

33. Stargazing

Keywords: courage, reaching for
the stars, what is truly possible

*It takes a lot of courage to reach for the stars
to expand the self, but it is possible.*

Look up to the starry skies and imagine how much we've already discovered of the myriad worlds out there. Humans have launched satellites into space to connect billions of people worldwide, and we've put men on the moon and sent rovers to Mars. We've created telescopes that are capable of seeing beyond our solar system and have discovered planets light years away. All of those things started as a spark in someone's imagination, little more than a passing thought that turned into life-changing history.

Knowing all this, ask yourself if what you want is truly impossible. Will it be difficult? Probably. Will it require you to grow, adapt, have courage and take risks? Yes, of course. But is it impossible? No, my dear, it is not. Something is only impossible until someone believes enough to make it a reality. There is a pathway for you to manifest your dreams and ideas if you're willing to reach higher than what you're comfortable with. You cannot reach your goals being who you are now and, while there's nothing wrong with who you are today, if you were the kind of person who could accomplish your goals you'd have them already. Have the audacity to imagine your best self and then become that.

How do you need to grow in order to chase your dreams: are there skills you need to learn or habits to defeat, or do you need to forgive someone and possibly yourself? Consider how you can expand yourself whether your reading is about love, career, finances or creative pursuits. You broaden your ideas of what's possible every time you have the courage to learn something new or challenge an outdated idea of yourself.

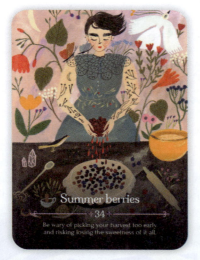

Summer berries

+ 34 +

Be wary of picking your harvest too early
and risking losing the sweetness of it all.

34. Summer berries

Keywords: ripening, sweetness, maturity

*Be wary of picking your harvest too early
and risking losing the sweetness of it all.*

We live in a fast world that was never meant to be so fast. It takes months for fruits and vegetables to reach maturity, and there is an important lesson to be learned by observing their growth. Your situation needs time to ripen just like summer berries. Pick your harvest too early and it may be sour, bitter or tough to chew, whereas patience is rewarded by a sweet bounty of juicy fruit.

You are on the right path but it will take more time before you reach your desired outcome, so use this time to tend to small tasks. A garden requires you to be watchful of weeds and pests, and you can apply the same logic to your goals. Employ practical actions such as getting organized or evaluating your progress to help you determine your next steps. Accept that this is the process and it is out of your control. Things will progress in the proper time, and any attempts to speed things along could leave you with undesirable results.

When this card appears you can trust that you are safely working towards your long-term goals and will find success. It may take longer than you'd like but nevertheless it will happen.

Summer solstice

+ 35 +

Like the sun, spread your ray of light
and ignite the light in others.

35. Summer solstice

Keywords: growth, good fortune, prosperity

*Like the sun, spread your ray of light
and ignite the light in others.*

The sun is finally shining down on you and that is reason to celebrate. When this card appears in your reading you can expect increase, good fortune and happy opportunities in all areas of your life, from money to love, recognition for your efforts to news of an addition to your family. You are receiving all of the hopes and dreams you have been working towards for a very long time. In fact, you might have such good favor that you cannot realistically keep it all to yourself and will feel moved to share it with your loved ones and community. This, in turn, plants the seeds for even more abundance.

The ability to provide for your family adds to the gratitude in your heart, attracting more joy and light. As your light grows so, too, do the opportunities available to you. Your energy and charisma become beacons for others to bask in the glow of your success and for even more successful people to see and reward your talents.

The shadow side to this card is the fear of losing all that you have gained. Enjoy your newfound wealth, knowing that your gratitude and faith in the universe will bring more increase rather than less. Don't ask "Why me?" or wait for the other shoe to drop, as this will attract the things you fear most. Instead, enjoy the fruits of your labor: sing, dance and shout your thanks to anyone who will listen.

Sunbathing

+ 36 +

The dance of stillness is calling for
you to live in its embrace.

36. Sunbathing

Keywords: spiritual strength, restoration

*The dance of stillness is calling for
you to live in its embrace.*

There are many ways to experience rest and self-care and you are being guided to explore the ways you need to heal at this time. Look beyond the most obvious choices of rest and relaxation, although these are worthy pursuits, because typically this card indicates a need to experience a spiritual restoration such as spending more time in meditation and prayer, communicating with your guides or ancestors or developing a spiritual self-care practice that might manifest in working with herbs, tarot cards, something related to your culture's mysticism or the natural cycles of the seasons.

It's important to establish a regular practice of spiritual nourishment rather than anything that is one-off. Having a ritual grounds your energy, allowing you to build your soul's strength, which will make it easier when you inevitably find yourself facing the harsh realities and responsibilities everyone faces throughout a lifetime.

Sun magick

✦ 37 ✦

Don't allow the power of your light to
scare you into dimming yourself.

37. Sun magick

Keywords: life, energy, vitality

*Don't allow the power of your light to
scare you into dimming yourself.*

You are coming into great alignment with your soul, and as a result you are literally shining brighter than ever before. Your energy and vitality are slowly growing, and you may even experience physical bursts of energy when this card comes into your reading. Your vibration is rising and you are pulling yourself out of the shadows you have recently experienced. If you are inquiring about a situation or recent challenge, pulling this card is your welcome sign that not only are things coming to a close but you will be victorious.

As a symbol of growth this card invites you to be noticed. Don't be afraid to let other people experience your energy: this is a positive card for those wishing to be in the public eye as it means you will be well received and, more than that, that people are already looking to you for guidance.

The shadow side of this card is the pressure to be all things for all people. Know that sharing your light does not mean you have to be on constant display. You are allowed to keep some things to yourself and no one should have total access to your energy, especially not for free. Don't be afraid to charge for what your energy and time are worth, which is true whether you are selling something physical such as a product or service or in your personal life among your family and friends. Relationships should be give and take. It is not your responsibility to loan your light to other people: they must learn to activate their own light so you can both bask in glory.

Sun salutation

⊹ 38 ⊹

Praise the temple that carries your
spirit. Support is needed.

38. Sun salutation

Keywords: wellness,
supporting your body

*Praise the temple that carries
your spirit. Support is needed.*

Receiving this card is an immediate call to make self-care a priority, especially if you have experienced struggles in manifesting more abundance or love into your life. It may not seem as though health and wellness have anything to do with your other goals, but consider that you would not have a way to experience wealth, joy, love or material possessions without your physical body. It is your soul's home and how you take in the world around you. Without vitality it could become much more difficult to show up for the things money affords you.

How can you enjoy travel, cars, houses or parties if you don't have the physical strength, or enjoy time with loved ones if your mind is foggy and tired? Often a healthy body results in a healthy brain, unlocking creative ideas and making it easier to problem solve and stimulate emotional wellness. You will find the solution or answer to your question with greater ease after making time for proper rest and better nutrition and taking a break.

There's no need to look a certain way or attempt to mold yourself to unrealistic beauty standards. All that's required is finding ways to support your body to facilitate a feeling of vitality, energy and strength. This will be different for different people, so listen to your body and let it guide you to what feels best.

Sunset dinner

+ 39 +

An invitation awaits you; yell to the
stars that you are ready to go!

39. Sunset dinner

Keywords: an invitation, a seat
at the table, leveling up

*An invitation awaits you; yell to
the stars that you are ready to go!*

You have been invited to the party and are about to receive your seat at the table. Your hard work is paying off, and the people who matter have noticed. Are you ready to shoot your shot? A new opportunity can come at any moment and you don't want to miss your chance to join the club. Do what you can to feel more confident and secure in the goals you are chasing: get that pitch together, dress for success and study or undertake research or anything else that is required to make you feel more prepared.

A second meaning of this card is the need to spend time with people who can lift you up. They say you are the same as the six people you spend the most time with, which is perfectly fine if those people represent where you want your life to go. However, if you're finding you are frustrated, disappointed or generally annoyed with the way your current circle of people are behaving then it might be time to find people who will push you out of your comfort zone and inspire you to be great.

I am ready affirmation

Repeat this affirmation seven times, and each time envision your intention and allow the words to sink into your body. You can change the words if you like; the point is to affirm to yourself what you want to bring forth:

> *I am ready for all that I desire.*
> *I am prepared to move forward.*
> *I am ready to acknowledge my worthiness.*
> *I am prepared to do what it takes.*
> *I am ready to accept.*
> *I am prepared to take action.*
> *I am ready.*

Sunstone

+40+

In the uniqueness of who you are
lives a world yet to be discovered.

40. Sunstone

Keywords: opportunities,
unexpected luck, fame

*In the uniqueness of who you are
lives a world yet to be discovered.*

Sunstone is a stone of success that shows you talents that are unique to you, draws good luck and increases your opportunities. Additionally, it stimulates leadership qualities, unlocking your ability to dance to the beat of your own drum. The lesson here is that when you are true to yourself success, fame and wealth naturally follow. Your greatest asset is that no one else on the planet is like you: you can do the same things as someone else in the exact same way and still the outcomes will be different because the people are different. Likewise, you can be the most talented person in the room, but someone who is willing to look silly if it means standing out is more likely to be noticed despite being less talented, educated or capable.

Successful people stand out from the crowd and the best way of doing that is letting your weirdness out to play. You are likely receiving this card because you're seeking recognition in some way such as putting yourself up for a promotion, looking for ways to increase customers or you're ready to start dating. Don't get lost in the

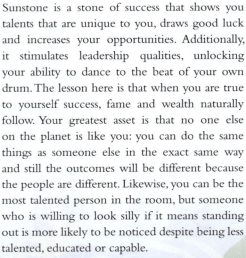

stream of familiarity by doing what everyone else is doing. Play close attention to those little details that set you apart and put them on display. Others will find these quirks to be endearing, intriguing, useful or downright entertaining – it doesn't really matter as long it leads you to the right opportunities.

Sun tea

+ 41 +

Slow, intentional, delicious interweaving with
life holds more magick than you think.

41. Sun tea

Keywords: slow magick,
calm living, simplicity

*Slow, intentional, delicious interweaving with
life holds more magick than you think.*

Sun tea is slow magick in the most delicious way possible: just fill a Mason jar with fruit and herbs and let the sun gently extract precious nutrients. It's the easiest form of folk healing, a wonderful way to nourish your body and mind. Whether you're doing it for physical or spiritual reasons, sometimes the biggest magick is found in the smallest acts of bliss.

Simplify, simplify, simplify: less is more when pulling the sun tea card. Don't make things harder than they need to be by introducing too many options, too many steps or too many people. In a world where everything is maxed out and amplified, this card advises you to keep things as uncomplicated as possible. Rather than focusing on doing more, scale back and do less really well. A chocolate cookie with brown butter, slowly aged whiskey, basil and artisanal sea salt sounds lovely but so does a good old-fashioned chocolate chip cookie baked to perfection. Adding extra layers is fine when the foundation is good, but otherwise it's just a busy mess that's all bark and no bite.

There's no rush to move things along faster than is necessary, so you can slow down and rest assured that you aren't missing out. Don't feel pressured to go out when you don't feel like it or to say "Yes" to an opportunity just because it's available. The whole world doesn't need to be famous or rich or eccentric or living life in the fast lane. No lifestyle is bad or wrong as long as it fulfills your needs.

Sun-tea recipe spell

This tea spell is ritualistic in how intentional the process is, and setting intentions into tea is a powerful way to work with the plant spirits of the ingredients to amplify your spell. Here we are also working with the sun's energy, which will boost your spell but, most importantly, the sun will bring you into your presence.

The recipe calls for regular teabags: use four bags for two quarts of water or eight bags for a gallon of water. I love hibiscus for this spell, but any herbal tea will work and you can even mix teabags. Glass is recommended over plastic for brewing sun tea, but if you're using plastic make sure the container doesn't contain any Bisphenol-A. You will need a glass container, some teabags, sprigs of lavender, edible flowers and sugar, honey or artificial sweetener.

This tea is flexible, and I suggest customizing it however works for you by replacing the lavender flowers with other flowers and choosing whether or not to sweeten the tea or add edible flowers. Customizing adds more of your magick, and the power comes in when you start the process. With everything you do, from preparing to drinking, keep your intention in mind.

Fill the container with water and place the teabags, lavender and flowers in it. Leave the container out in the sun to brew for two to three hours, then place it in the fridge to cool off. Once cool you can add the honey or sugar, and when you do so think of your intention again. Drink slowly, be present and enjoy.

Sun wheel

+42+

Make sure to catch your breath;
you are in for an unexpected journey.

42. Sun wheel

Keywords: movement,
adventure, taking action

Make sure to catch your breath;
you are in for an unexpected journey.

Be prepared: the presence of the sun wheel in a reading means things are about to speed up. You can expect a shift in movement in any number of ways — a project suddenly gaining significant traction, finding yourself on an adventure halfway across the world, a whirlwind romance or even the sudden urge to get up and move your physical body. This type of dynamic energy is exciting and generally stimulates positive outcomes, but change can be overwhelming — even good changes — so be sure to make time to catch your breath and plant your feet firmly on the ground.

Receiving this card is a sign to take action and get the ball rolling. It is a very good indication of success if you're willing to act quickly: even small steps taken at this time can stimulate significant leaps. Just be sure you know what you want before making any moves, as you don't want to find yourself with a plethora of opportunities only to realize you don't actually know where you're headed. The energy of the sun wheel is quick to come and quick to go, so don't waste it with indecision.

Wand making

· 43 ·

With a flick of focus you will come
to see a vision realized.

43. Wand making

Keywords: creation, directing
energy, manifestation

*With a flick of focus you will come
to see a vision realized.*

A wand is a ritualistic tool that is used to direct energy and also to summon energy, angels and deities. It's a way to connect with your desired outcome, opening a channel of manifestation from the spirit realm to you on earth.

This is a card of vision and focus on your desires. When it appears you may be looking ahead to your future, beginning to craft a clear understanding of what you want your life to look like in the coming days, months and even years. Receiving this card is your encouragement to hold this vision and direct all of your energy toward these goals, but keep your mind and eyes open. As you focus your intention on manifesting your dreams you'll find that the right opportunities and people will connect with your energy, offering exactly what you need to get ahead.

The last meaning of this card is that you are creating a stable position for yourself: the foundations are being laid for what will likely be a great success. Your confidence is growing, and with it your momentum. Keep up the good work, with your dreams front and center.

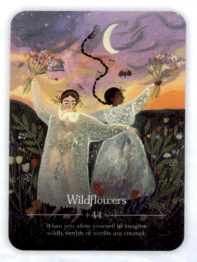

Wildflowers

+44+

When you allow yourself to imagine
wildly, worlds of worlds are created.

44. Wildflowers

Keywords: taking up space,
expansion, blooming

*When you allow yourself to imagine
wildly, worlds of worlds are created.*

There is no shortage of wildflowers to draw inspiration from. They come in every shape, color and size and blow in every direction, radiating expansive energy and blooming in every space they can fill. Your beauty and creativity are expansive as a wild meadow, and you have drawn this card to signal it's time to take up more space. Open your mind and let your ideas soar. You may do nothing with them, but just giving yourself room to imagine what is possible is enough to nourish your soul and stimulate your awakening.

This card alludes to a wonderful period of healing and blossoming, a time when all things begin to feel possible and you feel alive with vitality. You may find yourself in an especially fertile time, birthing fresh things into the world: a welcome sign for a new baby, engagement or the stirrings of a different project. Wildflowers encourages you to romanticize your life, bringing a nurturing, sensual quality to otherwise boring and mundane things.

Buy yourself flowers, perfume your home or use a whole Sunday for all-day self-care.

Celebrate the abundance all around you and look for ways to invite more beauty into your world. Mama Earth is an excellent place to start for inspiration.

About the authors

Lorriane Anderson is a multidisciplinary spiritual teacher, writer and soul-based entrepreneur whose work focuses heavily on intentional and energetic living as well as using spiritual practices as a pathway for profound healing, growth and transformation. She is the co-creator of the bestselling *Seasons of the Witch* oracle deck series along with several other titles in the spiritual space.

spiritelement.co
spiritelement

Juliet Diaz is an Indigenous Taino Cubana from a long line of bruja, medicine people and seers. She is a spiritual and literary activist and award-winning, bestselling author and the founder of Spirit Bound Press. She also represents the Indigenous Caribbean people with the Indigenous People's Movement, a global coalition that brings awareness on issues affecting Indigenous peoples and the planet.

Juliet has been featured in major publications such as *Oprah Magazine, The Atlantic, Wired, People Espanol, Mind Body Green* and *Refinery*. She was awarded outstanding author of the year, outstanding book of the year and outstanding deck of the year by the 2022 Witchcraft & Occult Media Awards. Her works include *Witchery: Embrace the Witch Within, Plant Witchery, The Altar Within, Seasons of the Witch* oracle series and *The Earthcraft Oracle*.

iamjulietdiaz.com

f **O** **y** **d** iamjulietdiaz

About the illustrator

Tijana Lukovic is based in the small medieval city of Gent in Belgium. Her paintings and illustrations are inspired by the magickal and metaphysical realms and contain traces of folklore, fairy tale and mythology and a love of nature. In her work Tijana shares her observations of the ever-changing seasons and her will to be more in tune with nature and the wheel of the year. She explores her inner mind and tries to bring deeply buried thoughts into the light. She is illuminating her unconscious mind and walking through the forest of her childhood memories. With her work she is on a journey to understand the complex universe of worlds inside and outside us. To follow her passion for drawing and painting Tijana earned an MFA in both fields. She loves to read and collect books but never has enough shelves.

tijanadraws.com

tijanadraws

Seasons of the Witch series

The *Seasons of the Witch* oracle series is coming along, and by the time we are done there will be eight decks, one for each sabbat on the wheel of the year. Already available are:

* Samhain
* Yule
* Beltane
* Mabon
* Imbolc

Coming soon is *Seasons of the Witch: Lammas Oracle*.

Don't forget to share your beautiful photos of the entire *Seasons of the Witch* oracle series and be sure to tag all the creators of this deck.

Bonus material

Scan the QR code below
to access exclusive bonus material for
The Season of the Witch Oracle-series.

SCAN ME